Improve Your Work-From-Home Life

Destiny S. Harris

. . .

Copyright

Copyright © 2024 Destiny S. Harris.

All rights reserved. No part of this publication may be reproduced without prior written permission from the author, except in the case of quotations.

Book design by Destiny S. Harris.

First printing edition 2024.

www.destinyh.com

. . .

...

A Gift For You

Thank you for taking the time to read this book. As a token of my appreciation, here is a gift to you.

I give away free books daily. Here's how to get your free books today:

Step 1: Visit

amazon.com/author/destinyharris

Step 2: Filter books by "Price: Low to High"

Step 3: Download available free eBooks

...

. . .

Table of Contents

. . .

. . .

Quick Bit

Thank you for taking the time to read this book.

My hope is that you leave at least 1% better than before you read this book and walk away with at least one takeaway.

I'd like to graciously ask that you help me by leaving a <u>review</u> of this book; your feedback helps me write better books and helps others get a glimpse of the book.

With Kindness,
Destiny

. . .

. . .

#1

Take a walk before your workday starts. If you work a job that has meetings, walk on your meetings.

You can also invite the people on the meeting to walk as well (maybe they'll be open to it). A lot can be accomplished when walking and you'll feel 100% more productive after the meeting since you got in extra steps.

...

. . .

#2

Part 1

Keep water on you at all times. Stay hydrated throughout your workday so you can keep your energy high and your mind sharp.

Part 2

Start your day with water versus caffeine.

. . .

. . .

#3

Batch your meetings together, leaving more time for thinking, strategic efforts, and relaxation.

...

...

#4

Eliminate unnecessary meetings or ask if your attendance is mandatory.

A lot of meetings are pointless. Make it a point to attend the ones you're absolutely needed in and obliterate the rest.

Remember, much work can be completed async, and more meetings don't equal higher productivity.

The more meetings you have, the less productive you often are.

...

. . .

#5

Meal prep.

Save time throughout your workdays by prepping your meals for the week.

Lunch can be put together quickly when your food is already prepped.

. . .

. . .

#6

Avoid gossip and pointless casual conversations. It's nice to have coffee chats here and there with coworkers, but if the conversations are turning into gripe or gossip sessions, you're wasting your time and mental/emotional energy.

Keep your productivity levels and mood elevated by avoiding unproductive communication.

...

. . .

#7

Keep a to-do list and put it on your calendar. I love the calendar to-do list because it allocates a specific time to a specific task.

Running to-do lists work great, too, but that will all depend on when you have time.

If you have a task, insert it into your calendar so you can allocate time to complete it without any intervention from meetings or other coworkers.

. . .

. . .

#8

Work in a clean environment.

Keep your desk and surrounding work area clean and ideal for your highest productivity.

Get rid of the plates, trash, clutter, and all the unnecessary so you can focus on your work.

. . .

. . .

#9

Work with natural light.

If possible, try to position your desk in a place that has natural light. It's good for the soul and your mood.

...

. . .

#10

Take breaks to workout, eat, breathe, read, walk, and care for yourself.

I use my lunchtime as my workout time. I can eat in a meeting, and if people don't want to see you eat, turn your camera off or raise the camera to a level that covers your mouth.

The one person who will look out for you better than anyone else is yourself. Be sure you prioritize your mental, emotional, physical, spiritual, and professional well-being.

...

. . .

Thank You For Reading

Thank you for reading this book.

Stay loved, blessed, lucky, favored, aware, joyous, enlightened, and committed to bettering yourself.

. . .

. . .

The End.

...

...

About Destiny S. Harris

Destiny S. Harris' goal is to positively inspire, cultivate, elevate, and educate the minds of individuals across the globe through her writing.

Creating (whether books, courses, articles, poetry, or music) has always been Destiny's thing, not to mention health & fitness and all things entrepreneurial.

Destiny published her first book, "Beauty Secrets for Girls," at age 11 and her second book, "Don't Wait Until It's Too Late," at age 12.

Destiny obtained three degrees in Psychology, Political Science, & Women's Studies. She also started her own music teaching business at the age of 14, which she led for over ten years. In addition, she has been teaching academic, career, and personal development topics to thousands of students and readers since 2004.

Outside of writing, Destiny loves and enjoys many activities: reading, weightlifting, walking, biking, traveling, football (and sports in general), dogs, animals, food, classic movies, quality and new experiences, mountain and ocean views, sleeping, plants, and nature.

Check out her work, leave a review, share your thoughts with your friends and family, and participate in a movement: **Serving others through self-education (books).**

<u>Complete the Steps To Get Free eBooks:</u>

Step 1: Go to

amazon.com/author/destinyharris

Step 2: Filter books by "Price: Low to High"

Step 3: Download available free books

...

...

Connect W/ Destiny S. Harris

Please reach out and stay in touch. Start a conversation today @ destinyh.com

. . .

. . .

Free Gifts!

Access courses & free eBooks at the link below:

destinyh.com

. . .

Please Leave A Review

If this book impacts you in some way, please let me know by dropping a review on it.

I write better books with **your** input.

. . .

Tell Me What You Want

I've written many books, but if you don't see what you're looking for or need, get in touch with me via my website, articles, comments, or reviews, and let me know what you're looking for so I can create it for you. I'm here to serve.

Destiny

. . .

. . .

www.ingramcontent.com/pod-product-compliance
Lightning Source LLC
Chambersburg PA
CBHW031425250726
48656CB00002B/829